MICHAEL FEINSTEIN

only one
the songs of jimmy webb

ISBN 0-634-06766-4

HAL•LEONARD®
CORPORATION

7777 W. BLUEMOUND RD. P.O. BOX 13819 MILWAUKEE, WI 53213

Visit Hal Leonard Online at
www.halleonard.com

AFTER ALL THE LOVES/
ONLY ONE LIFE

Words and Music by
JIMMY WEBB

Slowly, with freedom

With pedal

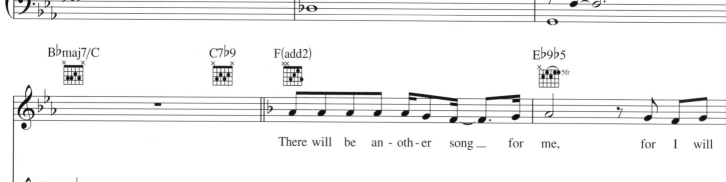

There will be an-oth-er song ___ for me, for I will

molto rit.   *a tempo*

sing   it.

There will be an-oth-er dream ___ for

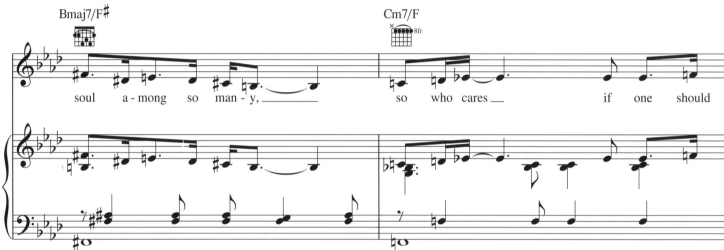

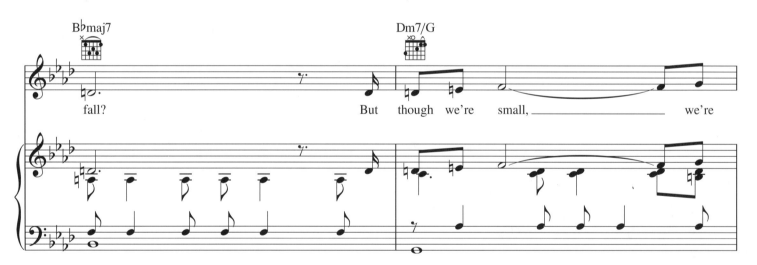

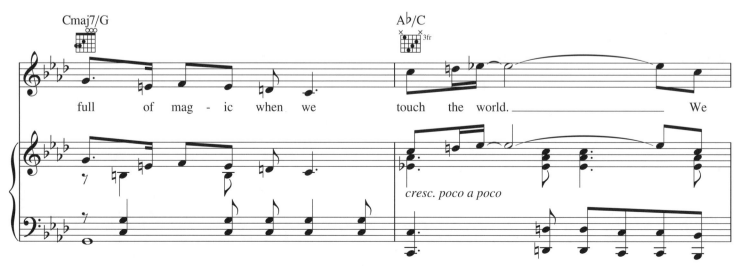

DIDN'T WE

Words and Music by
JIMMY WEBB

BELMONT AVENUE

Music and Lyrics by
JIMMY WEBB

It's twelve o - 'clock _____ and all is well
At twelve o - 'clock _____ we say is fare - well

on Bel - mont _ Av - e - nue. _____
with kiss - es _ sweet and free. _____

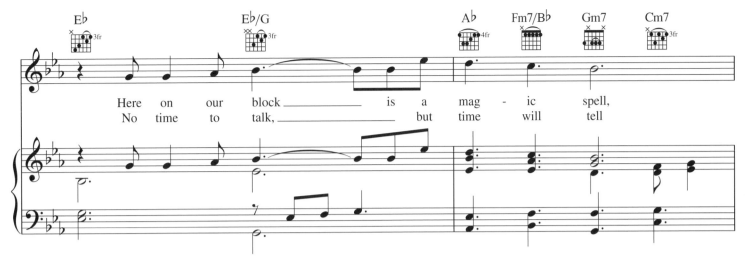

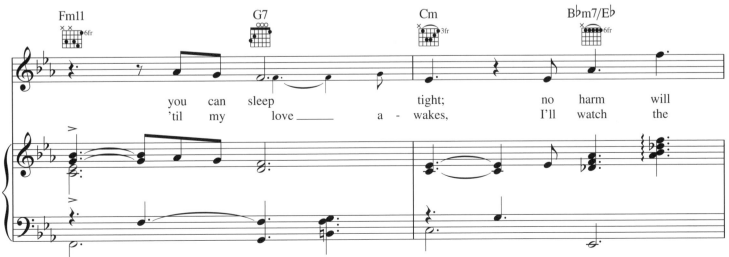

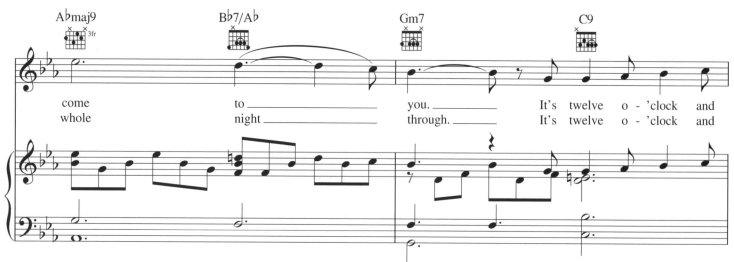

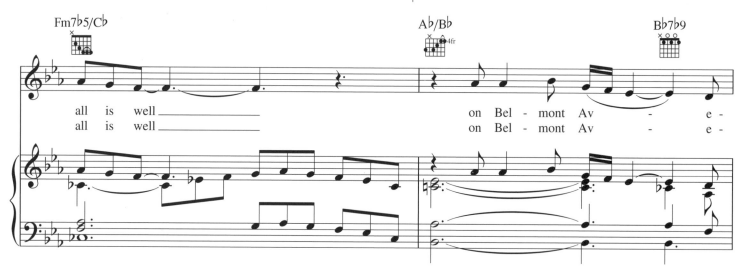

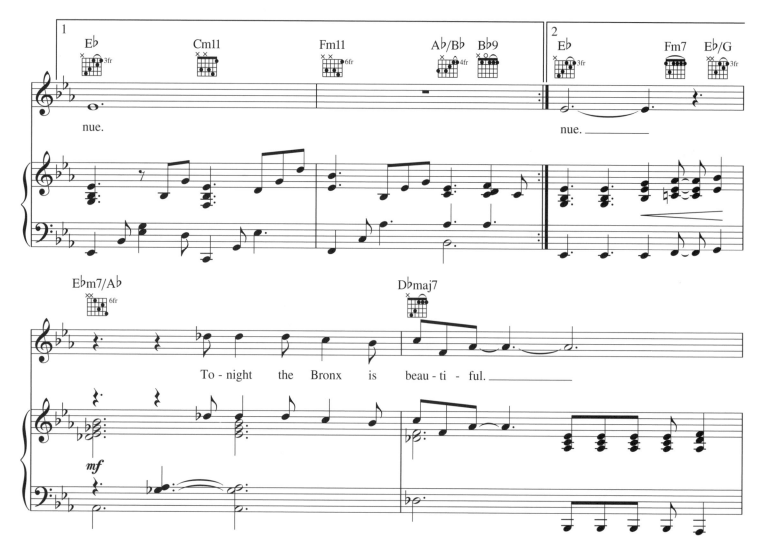

it plays a clos - ing tune, as in the dark _____ we

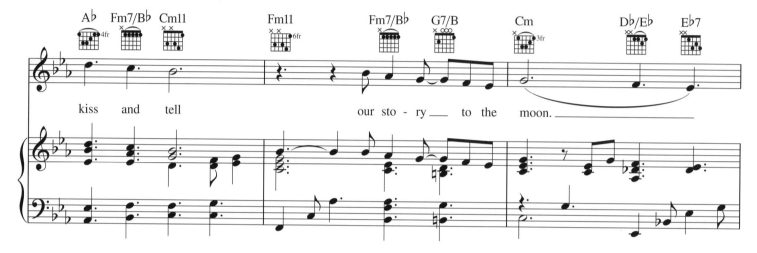

kiss and tell our sto - ry _____ to the moon. _____

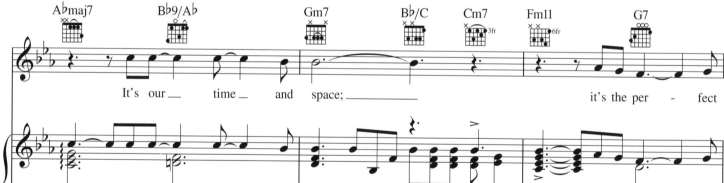

It's our _____ time _____ and space; _____ it's the per - fect

place to watch these dreams come true. _____ It's twelve o - 'clock and

UP, UP AND AWAY

Words and Music by
JIMMY WEBB

beau - ti - ful— bal - loon?——
beau - ti - ful— bal - loon.——
beau - ti - ful— bal - loon.——

We could float a - mong— the stars—
We can sing a song— and sail—
If you'll hold my hand— we'll chase—

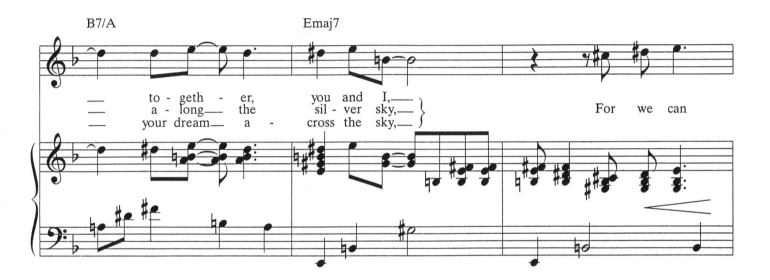

— to - geth - er, you and I,—
— a - long— the sil - ver sky,—
— your dream— a - cross the sky,—

For we can

fly!

Up, up and a - way,_____ in my beau - ti - ful,_____ my

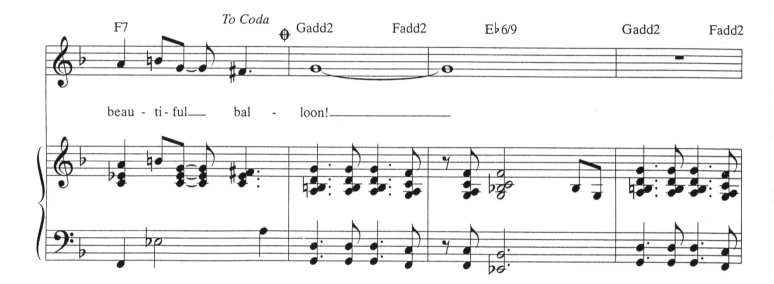

beau - ti - ful_____ bal - loon!_____

The

Sus - pend - ed un - der a twi - light

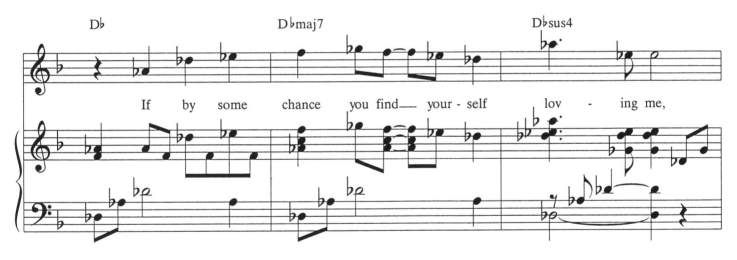

24

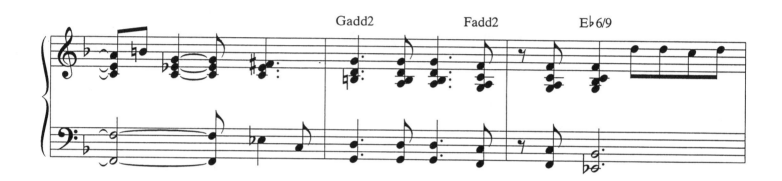

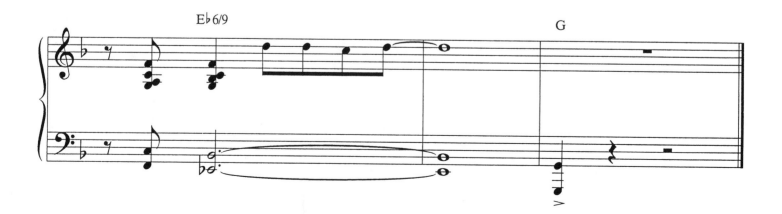

SHE MOVES AND EYES FOLLOW

Words and Music by
JIMMY WEBB

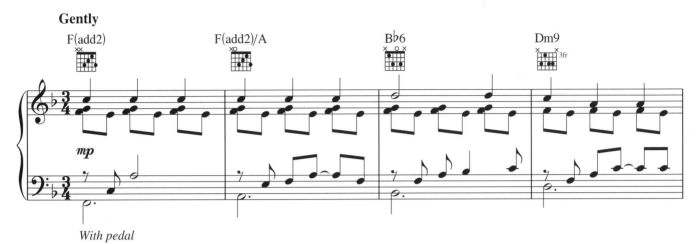

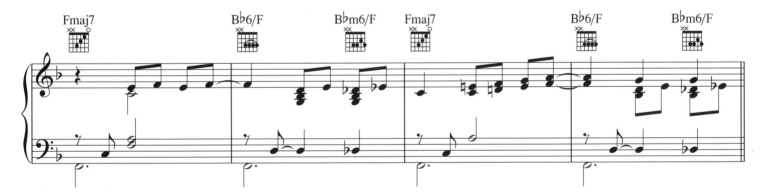

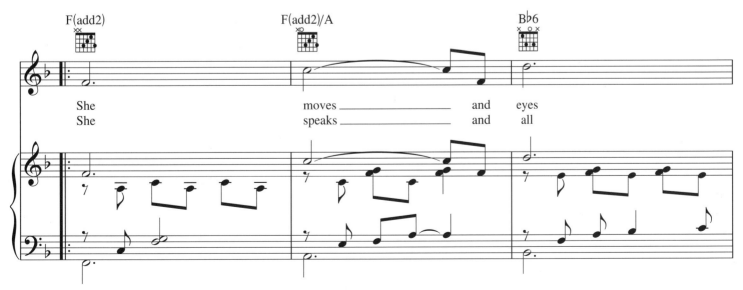

She moves _____ and eyes
She speaks _____ and all

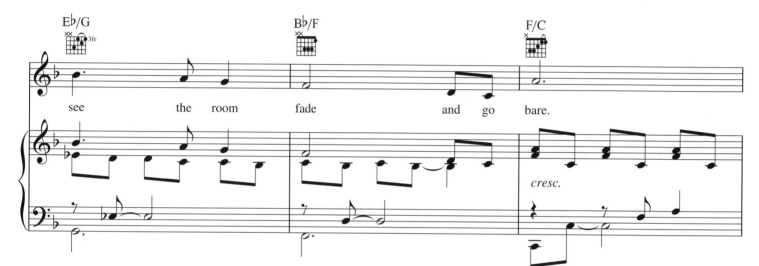

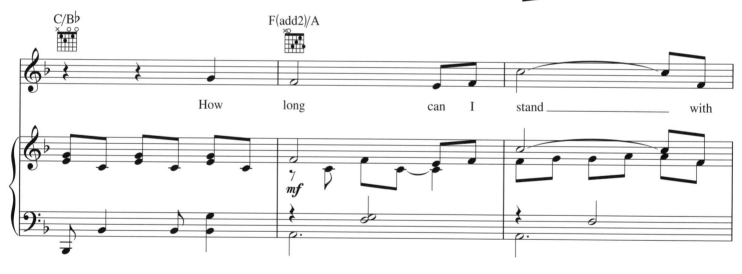

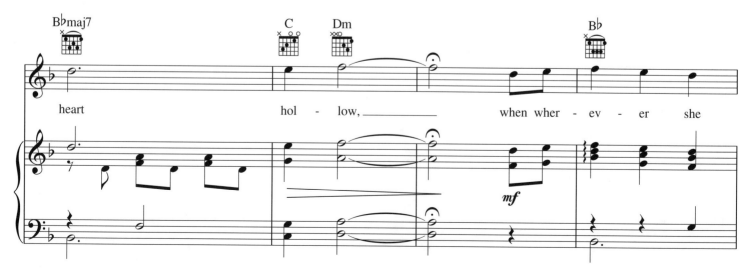

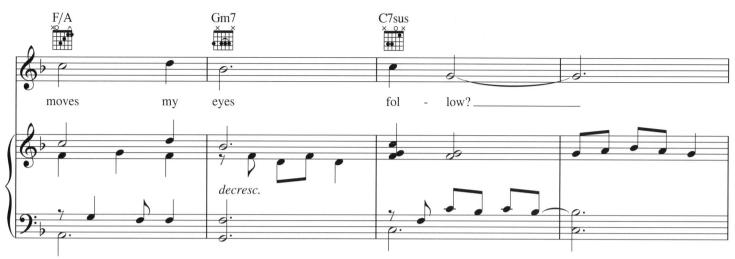

moves   my   eyes   fol - low? _____

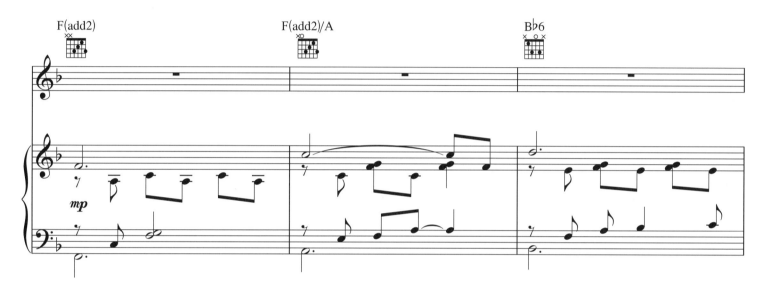

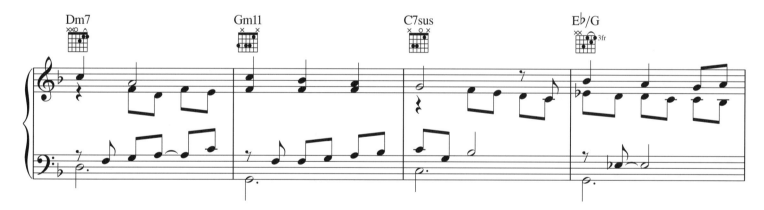

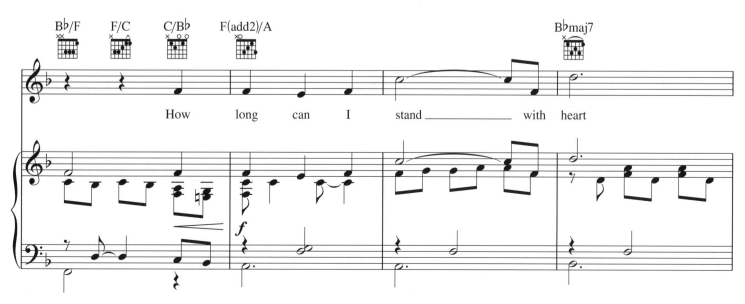

How   long   can   I   stand _____ with   heart

Freely

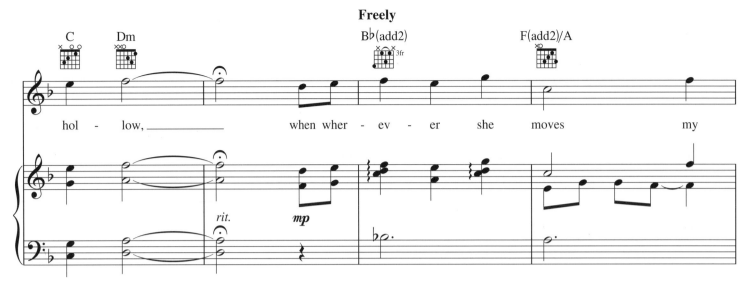

hol - low, _____ when wher - ev - er she moves my

eyes fol - low _____ her _____

there? _____

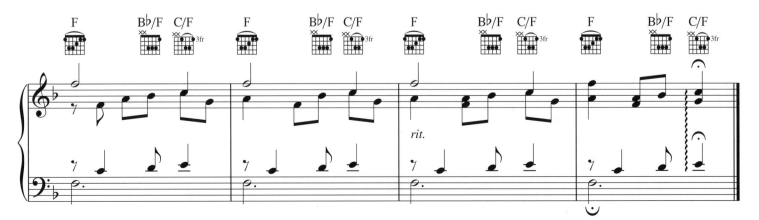

ALL I KNOW

Words and Music by
JIMMY WEBB

Moderately slow

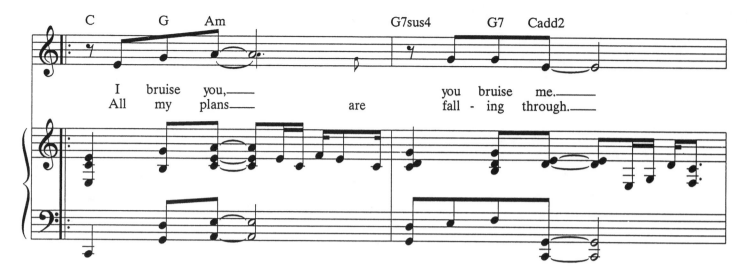

I bruise you,_____ you bruise me._____
All my plans_____ are fall - ing through._____

We both bruise_____ too eas - i - ly,_____ too eas - i - ly_____ to
All my plans_____ de - pend on you,_____ de - pend on you_____ to

let it show;_____ I love you,_____ and that's all I
help them grow._____ I love you_____ and that's all I

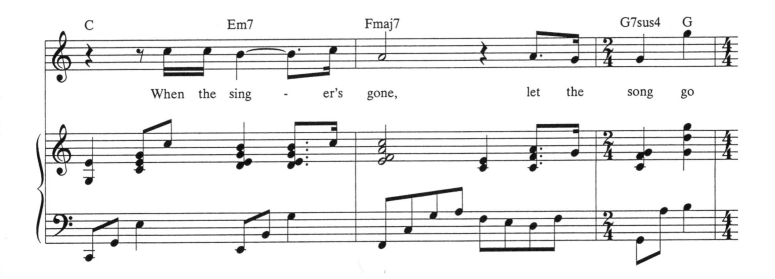

dawn._____ In the dark-est night_____ there's a light be-yond._____

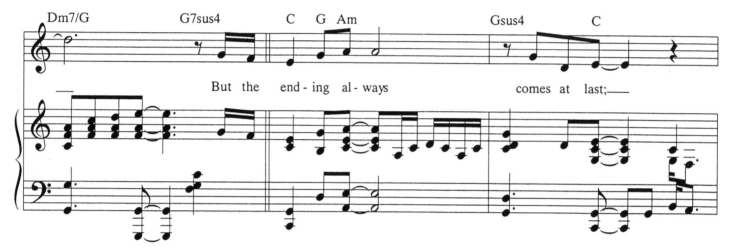

But the end-ing al-ways comes at last;___

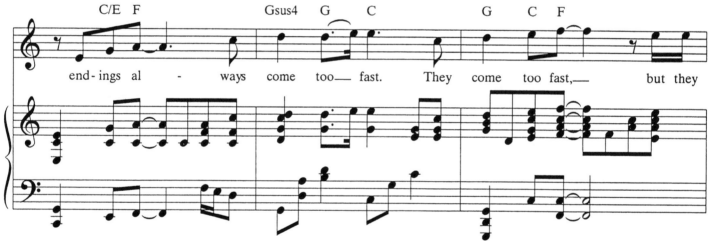

end-ings al - ways come too__ fast. They come too fast,___ but they

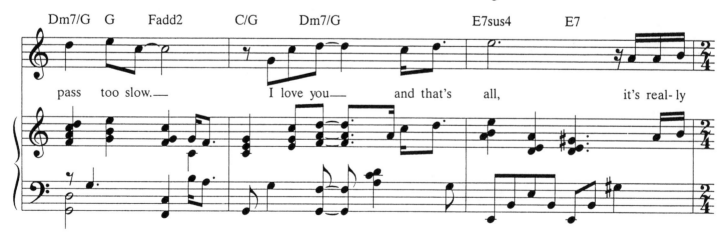

pass too slow.___ I love you___ and that's all, it's real-ly

THE MOON IS A HARSH MISTRESS

Words and Music by
JIMMY WEBB

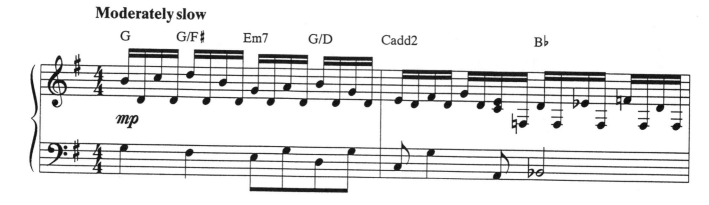

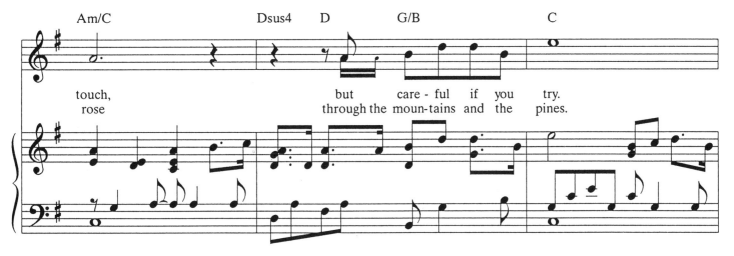

touch,
rose

but care-ful if you try.
through the moun-tains and the pines.

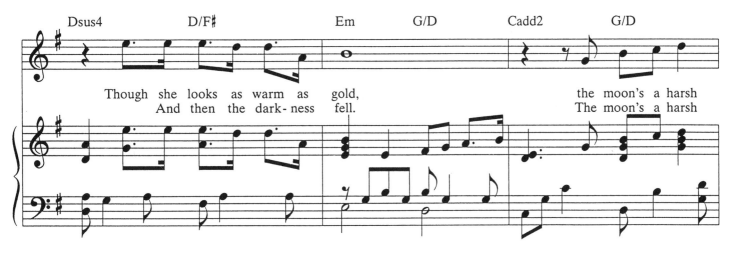

Though she looks as warm as gold,
And then the dark-ness fell.

the moon's a harsh
The moon's a harsh

mis - tress.
mis - tress;

The moon can be so cold.
it's hard to love her well.

Once the sun did

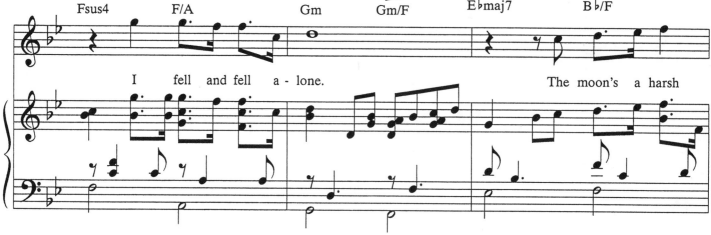

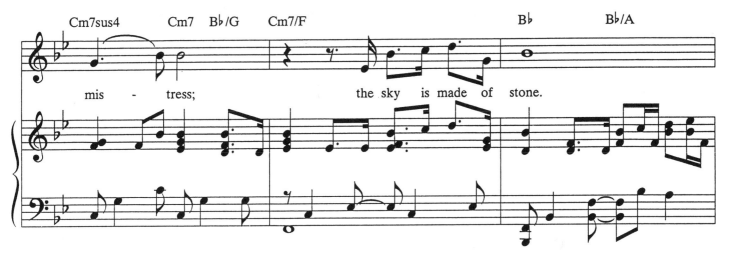

mis - tress; the sky is made of stone.

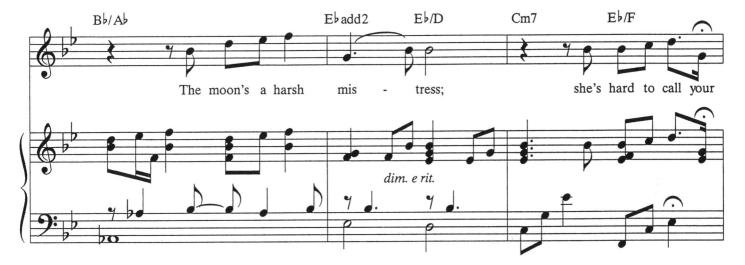

The moon's a harsh mis - tress; she's hard to call your

own.

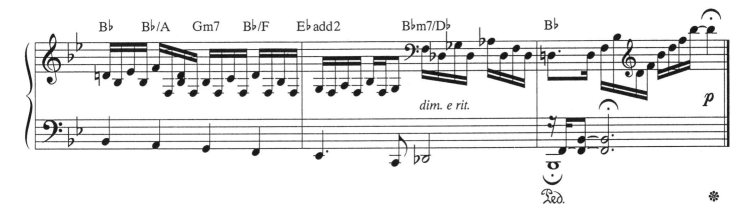

ADIOS

Words and Music by
JIMMY WEBB

Moderately slow

Ran a-way from home____ when I was sev-en-teen____ to be with you____

Go-ing up____ north____ where the hills are win-ter green,____ I have to leave you____

on the Cal-i-for-nia coast.____

on the Cal-i-for-nia coast.____

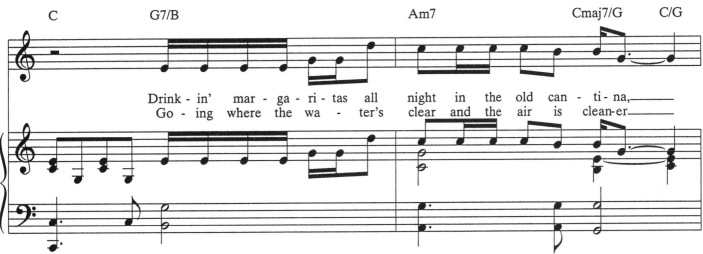

Drink - in' mar - ga - ri - tas all night in the old can - ti - na,
Go - ing where the wa - ter's clear and the air is clean - er

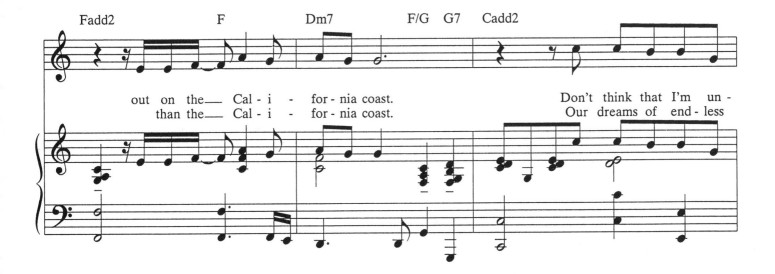

out on the___ Cal - i - for - nia coast.
than the___ Cal - i - for - nia coast.

Don't think that I'm un -
Our dreams of end - less

grate - ful,___
sum - mer___

and___ don't look so mo - rose.___
were___ just too gran - di - ose.___

A - di -

SKYWRITER

Words and Music by
JIMMY WEBB

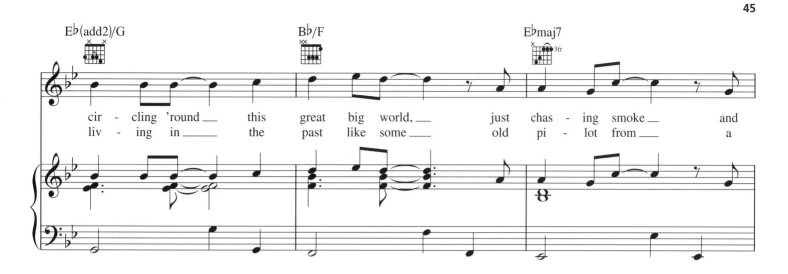

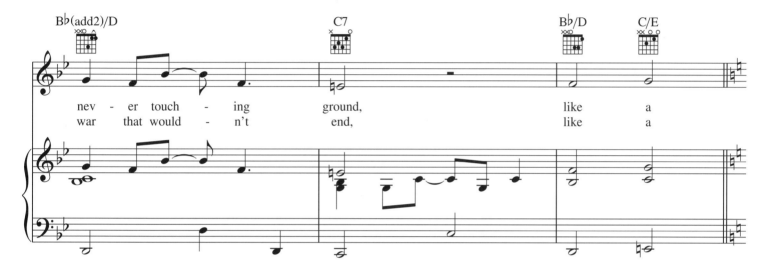

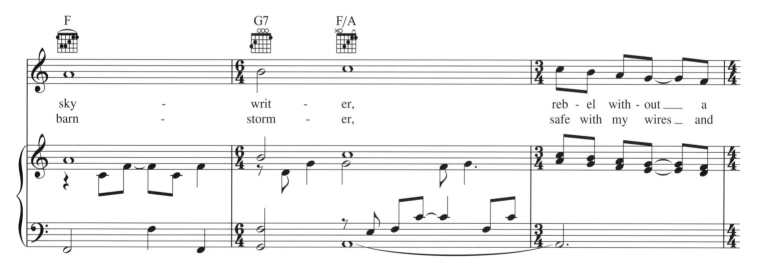

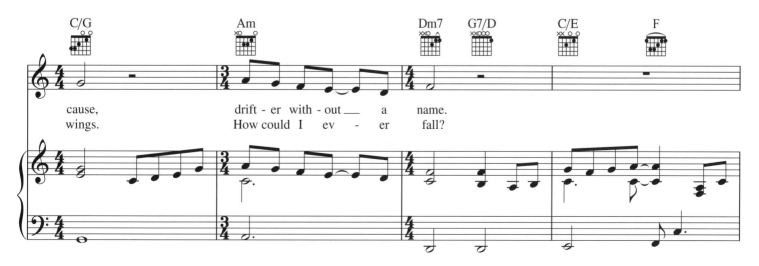

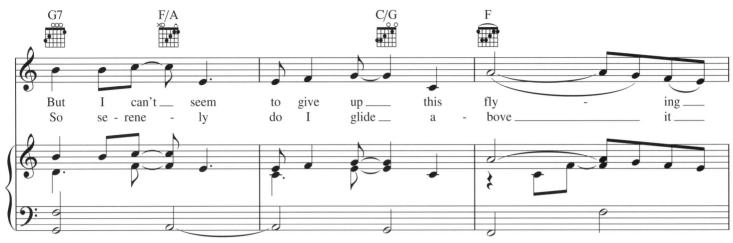

But I can't __ seem to give up __ this fly - ing __
So se - rene - ly do I glide __ a - bove _____ it __

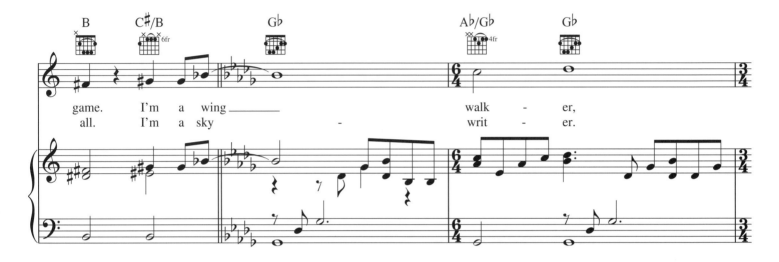

game. I'm a wing __ walk - er,
all. I'm a sky - writ - er.

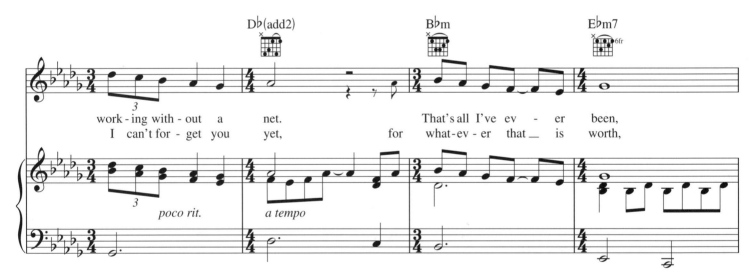

work - ing with - out a net. That's all I've ev - er been,
I can't for - get you yet, for what - ev - er that __ is worth,

poco rit.   *a tempo*

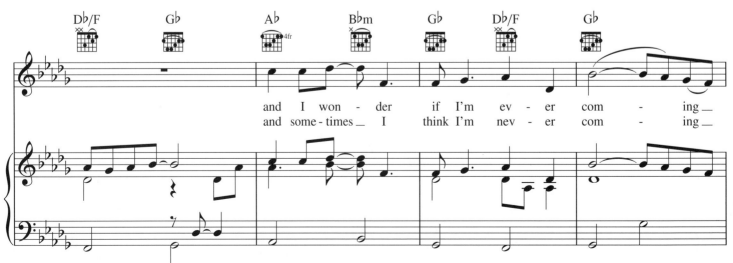

and I won - der if I'm ev - er com - ing __
and some - times __ I think I'm nev - er com - ing __

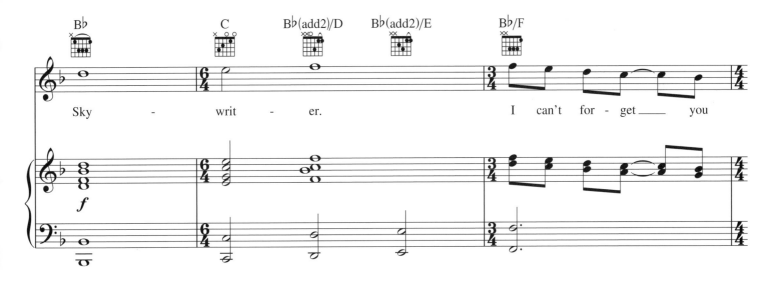

and some-times __ I think I'm nev - er com - ing __

back to _____ earth. _____
(Vocal 1st time only)

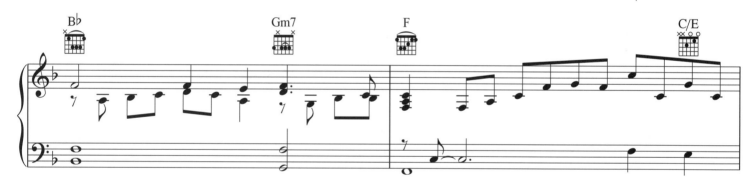

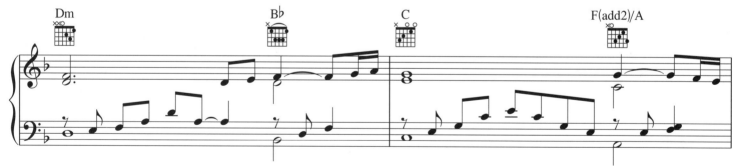

IS THERE LOVE AFTER YOU

Music and Lyrics by
JIMMY WEBB

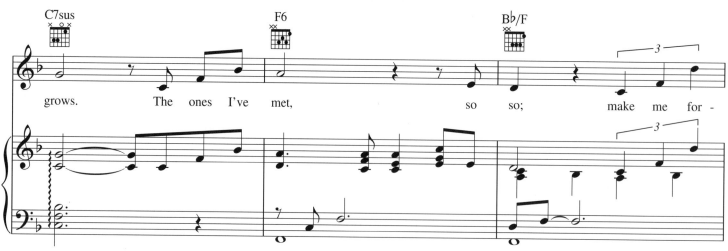

grows. The ones I've met, so so; make me for-

get? Hell, no, and it's so bor-ing here on the

ground, af - ter the soar-ing. ___ We were

soar - ing. ___ And I

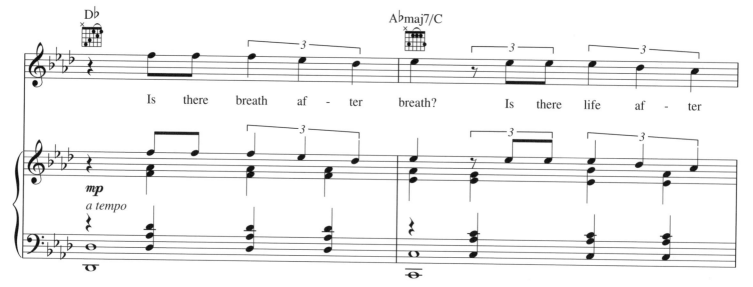

Is there breath af - ter breath? Is there life af - ter

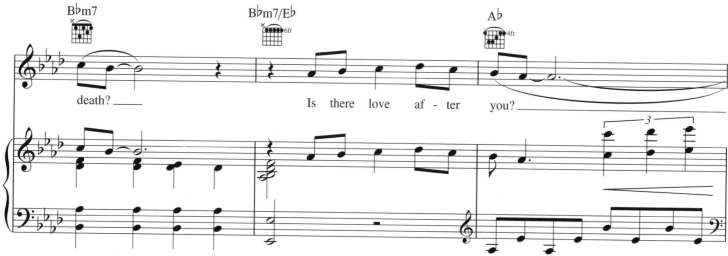

death? ____ Is there love af - ter you? ____

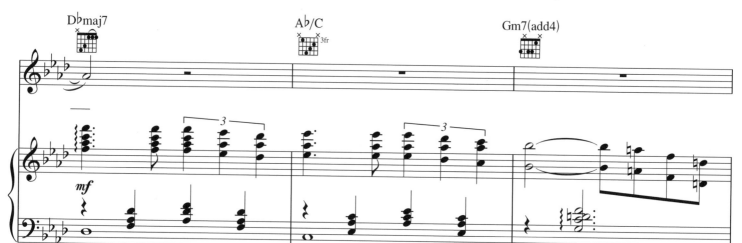

Am I per - plexed? I swear. What hap - pens

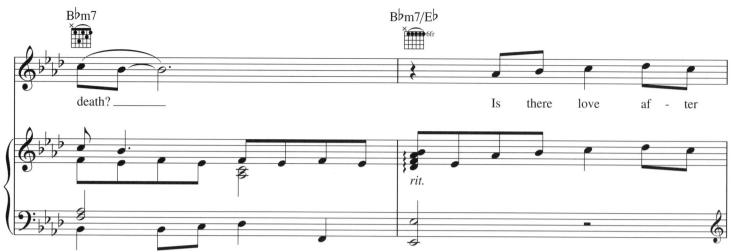

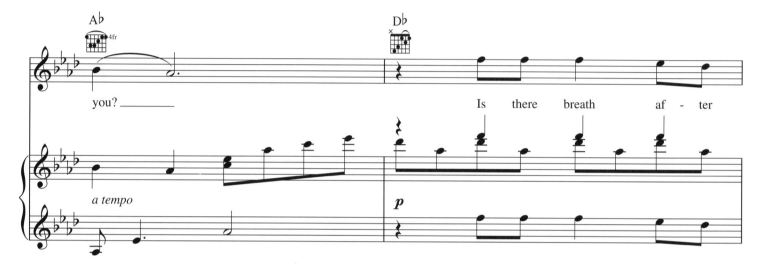

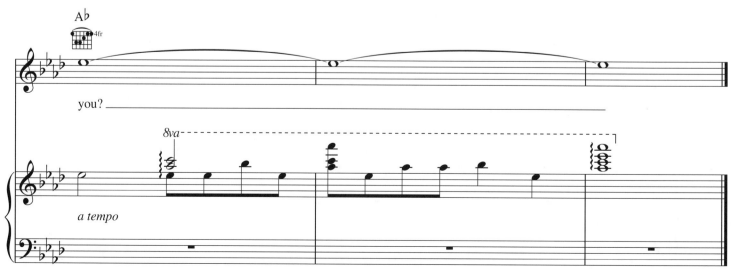

LOUISA BLU

Music and Lyrics by
JIMMY WEBB

Moderately slow, with freedom

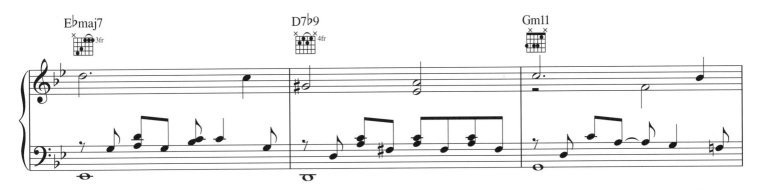

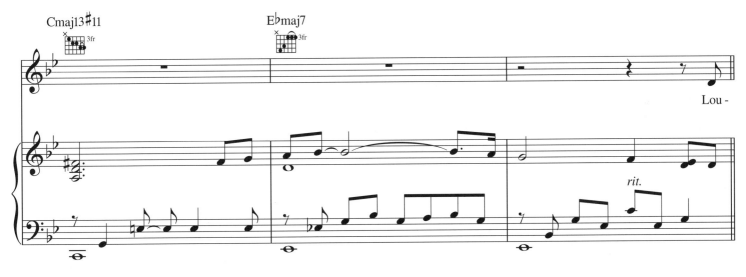

Lou-
i - sa Blu, is there a lit - tle girl in - side of you,

but there are those _____ who claim that her

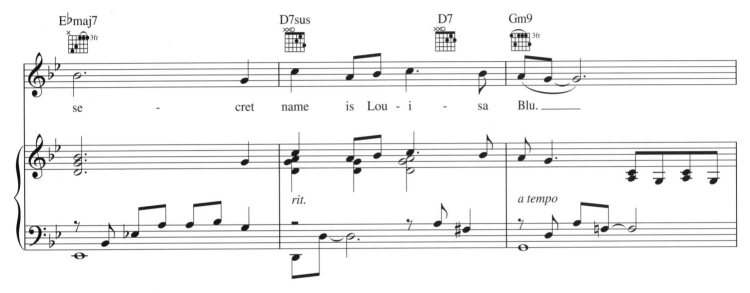

se - cret name is Lou - i - sa Blu. _____

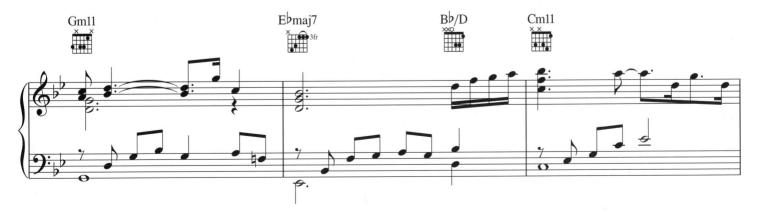

TIME FLIES

Words and Music by
JIMMY WEBB

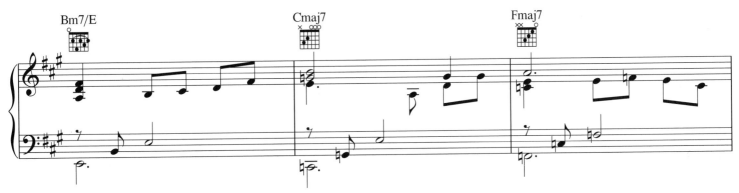

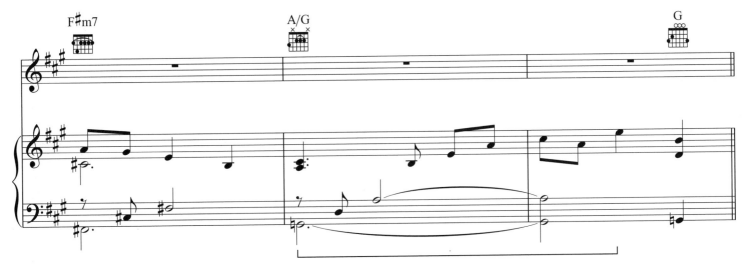

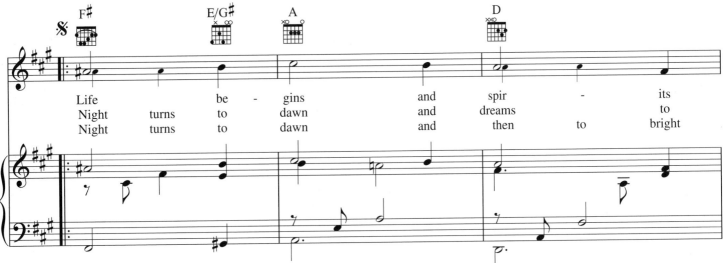

Life be - gins and spir - its
Night turns to dawn and dreams then to bright
Night turns to dawn and dreams then to bright

rise,   and   they   be - come   mem - 'ries   that   va - por -
sighs,   and   sighs   change   to   sweet   love   that   nev - er
skies,   and   bright   skies   to   pic - nics   on   warm   Ju -

ize   and   the   va - por   be - comes   the   dreams   we   de -
dies   and ___ love   be - comes   laugh - ter   and   lull - a -
lys,   to ___ deep   um - ber   au - tumn   and   win - ter   good -

To Coda ⊕

vise,
bies, }   and   while   we   are   dream - ing, ___   time
byes,

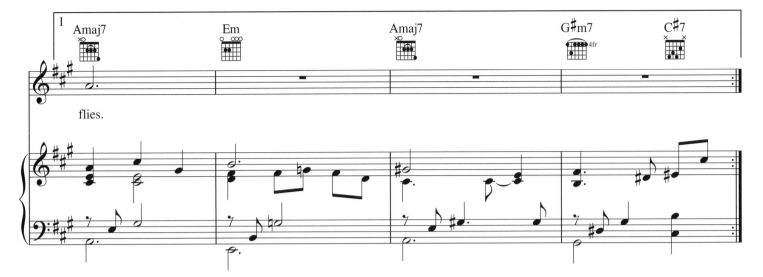

flies.

flies. While we are dream - ing we meet and ex -

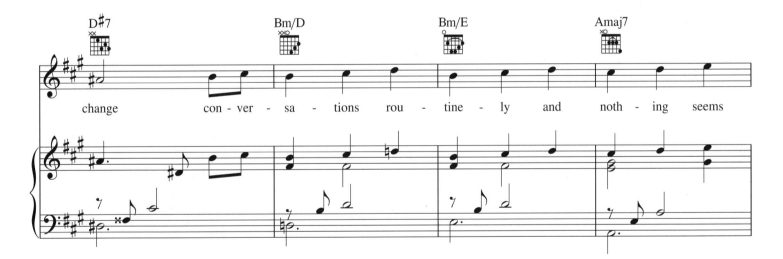

change con - ver - sa - tions rou - tine - ly and noth - ing seems

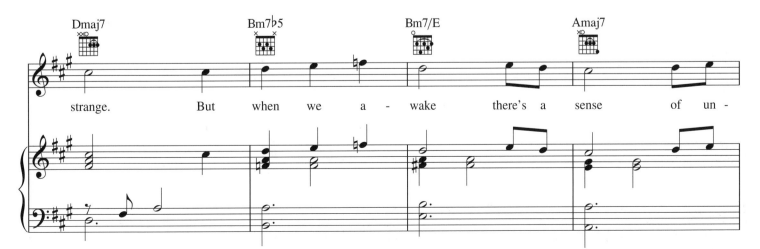

strange. But when we a - wake there's a sense of un -

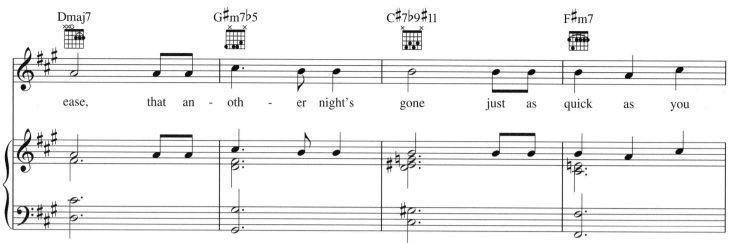

ease, that an - oth - er night's gone just as quick as you

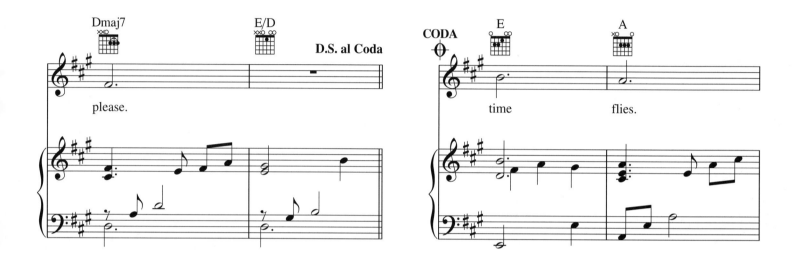

please.

D.S. al Coda

CODA

time flies.

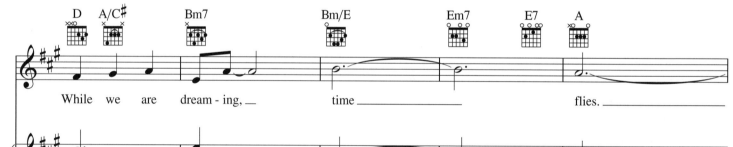

While we are dream - ing, __ time ___ flies. __

THESE ARE ALL MINE

Words and Music by
JIMMY WEBB

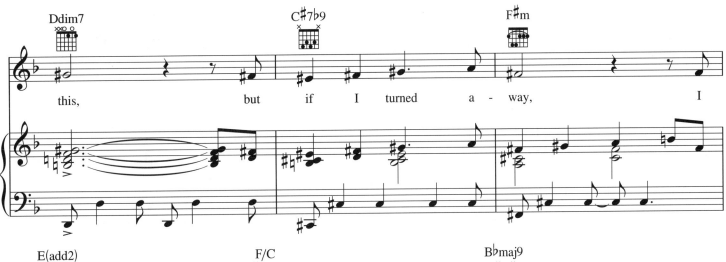

this, but if I turned a-way, I

know I'd miss your kiss, blown so ___ care - less -

ly, I'd catch and save for me, and when I

dream my fine deep sleep, these are all mine to keep. ___

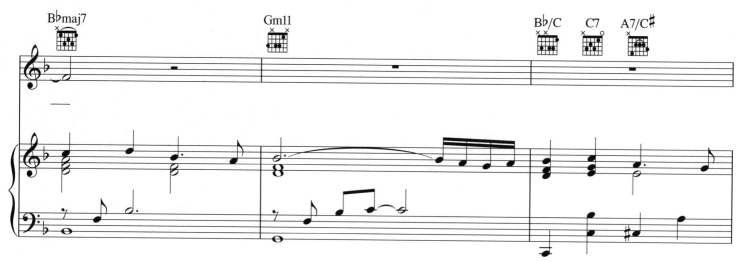

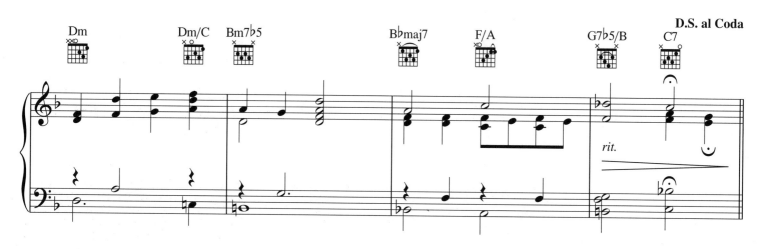

D.S. al Coda

CODA

me, and when I dream my fine deep sleep, these

are all mine, _____ these are all mine to

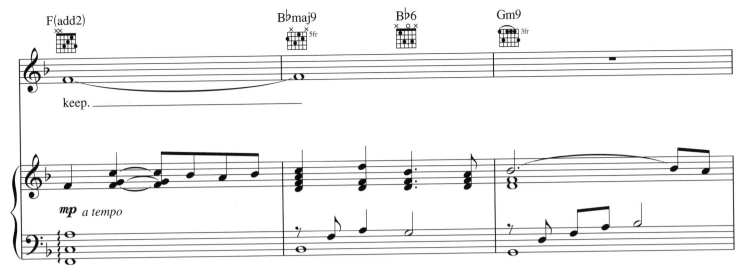

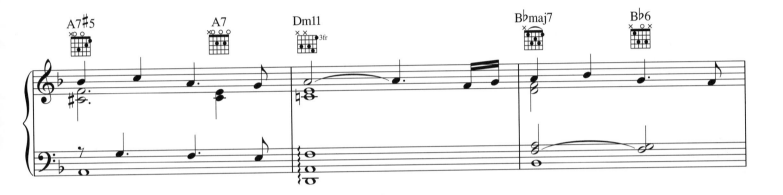

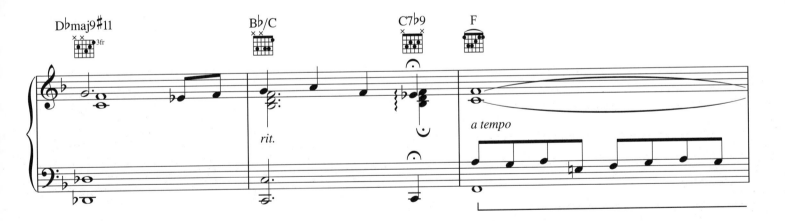

PIANO

Words and Music by
JIMMY WEBB

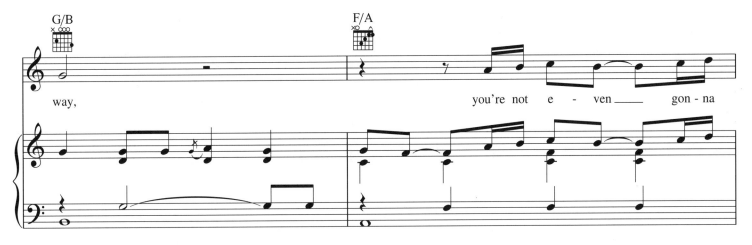

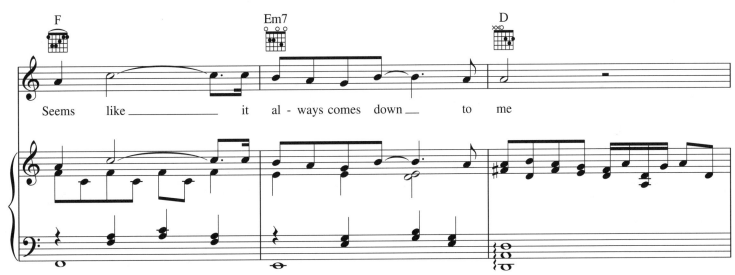

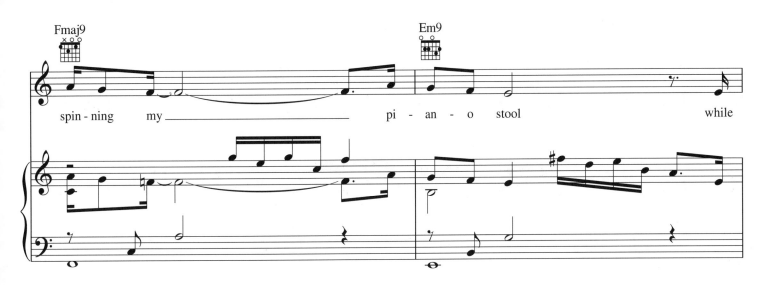

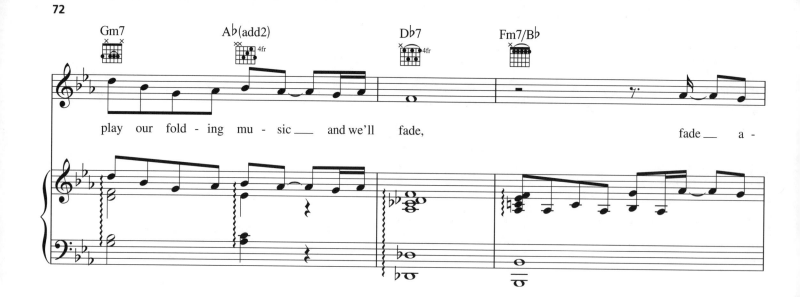

play our fold - ing mu - sic ___ and we'll fade, fade ___ a -

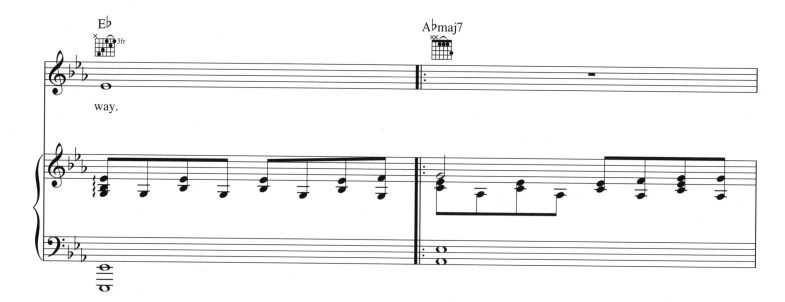

way.

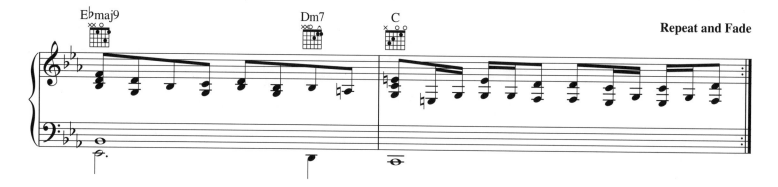

Repeat and Fade

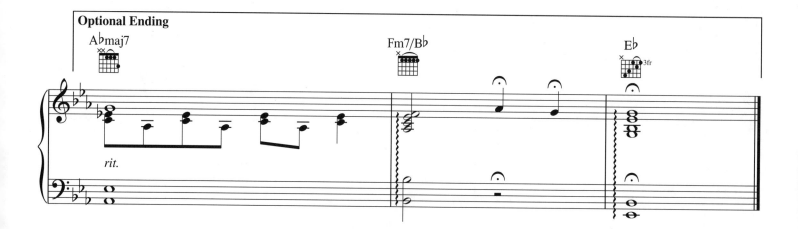

Optional Ending

rit.